Her cold eyes

ISBN-10: 1492310751

ISBN-13: 978-1492310754

Her cold eyes

The adolescent

vampire's songbook

Poems

by

Peter Hardcastle

DEDICATION

This book is dedicated to my
beloved daughter Aglaia
who passed away to early.

Content

The glorious life of Martha G.

Since Martha G. was a neat young girl
with sweet eyes and red lips
all the guys wanted her to be their lover.
Her mama had an eye on Marta G.
so that she didn`t warm their beds an be
their cover.

She lived a glorious life,
the short life of Martha G.

One day her mother had another lover,
a fat guy named Toddy-Loo.
And Martha`s mam said: "Listen, darling
mine,
Toddy has an eye on you,
be careful, don`t warm his bed and be his
cover!"

She lived a glorious life,
the short life of Martha G.

One day her mother went to work,
the door clapped one past ten,
and Martha G. was all alone and crying.
With Toddy-Loo, her mother`s lover,
she warmed their bed, he was her loving
cover.

She lived a glorious life,
the short life of Martha G.

Martha G. was thrown out of the door,
pregnant like a swine to slaughter,
she came down, dying at the rivers floor,
giving up her heart to the icy water,
and her mother kissed her lover, was his
loving cover.

She lived a glorious life,
the short life of Martha G.

Good bye Sammy

Hey gimme me that cadillac,
I wanna drive my baby
down to sunset boulevard.

Hey gimme me that red hat,
I wanna drive my baby
down to sunset boulevard.

Dance, dance, dance,
I'm Sam the hip.

Hey give me ten thousend bucks,
I wanna drive my baby
down to sunset boulevard.

Hey give me that golden ring
I wanna drive my baby
down to sunset boulevard.

Dance, dance, dance,

I'm Sam the hip.

Hey give me all you have,
I wanna drive my baby
down to sunset boulevard.

Hey give me your warm laugh,
I wanna drive my baby
odown to sunset boulevard.

Dance, dance, dance,
I'm Sam the hip.
Dance, dance, dance,
I'm Sam the hip.

Fly me to the moon

Hey baby, tonight we're dancing,
my love, and we're singing
it to the friendly moon.

Fly me to the moon,
my love,
fly me to the moon.

Hey baby, tonight we are kissing
my love, and we're giving
it to the friendly moon

Fly me to the moon,
my love,
fly me to the moon.

Hey baby, tonight we are celebrating,
my love, and we're dedicating
it to the friendly moon.

Fly me to the moon,
my love,
fly me to the moon.

Hey baby, tonight you were missing,
my love, and i`m crying
it to the friendly moon

Fly me to the moon,
my love,
fly me to the moon.

Hey baby, I miss your sweet caress
my love, I must confess
it to the friendly moon

Fly me to the moon,
my love,
fly me to the moon.

Lonesome man

Under the burning sun
His ship was wrecked
his pals were drowned
and he was all alone
under the burnig sun.

Don`t give up, Robinson Crusoe,
don`t give up your soul!

Under the burning sun
on the island`s beach
a man slept silent
his hopes were gone
Under the burning sun.

Don`t give up, Robinson Crusoe,
don`t give up your soul!

Under the burning sun
he found his knife,

he fetched his gun,
and began to struggle,
under the burning sun.

Don`t give up, Robinson Crusoe,
don`t give up your soul!

Under the burning sun,
he built his house
he grew his corn
and found a friend
under the burning sun.

Don`t give up, Robinson Crusoe,
don`t give up your soul!

Under the burning sun,
he said to Friday:
"I reach for home!"
He felt lonesome still,
under the burning sun.

Don`t give up, Robinson Crusoe,

don`t give up your soul!

Under the burning sun,
a ship reached the isle
and fetched him up,
he left his life
under the burning sun.

Don`t give up, Robinson Crusoe,
don`t give up your soul!

Under the burning sun,
his legend still lives
his hope gives strength
to every lonesome man
under the burning sun.

Don`t give up, Robinson Crusoe,
don`t give up your soul!

Undercover agent

I'm just an undercover agent
i`m fighting every night
and every bloody day,
I`m just an undercover agent.

I shot that man, and he shot back,
her lips so sweet, her eys so black,
I couldn`t aks her why
that poor guy had to die.

I'm just an undercover agent
i`m fighting every night
and every bloody day,
I`m just an undercover agent.

Last night she lost her lover,
I tore away his sticky cover,
the bullet blew his head
he fell down bleading dead.

I'm just an undercover agent
i`m fighting every night
and every bloody day,
I`m just an undercover agent.

I took her home, I kissed her lips,
she cast me out, I missed her hips,
she laughed behind the door,
I spit my blood on the floor.

I'm just an undercover agent
i`m fighting every night
and every bloody day,
I`m just an undercover agent.

The next day they found her dead,
her sweet lips were poisoned blue
her cold eyes were blind
I felt no pity in my mind.

I'm just an undercover agent
i`m fighting every night
and every bloody day,

I`m just an undercover agent.

So many Years have gone by,
but still her lips are blue
and I see her cold blind eyes
in my bloody nightmare dreams.

I'm just an undercover agent
i`m fighting every night
and every bloody day,
I`m just an undercover agent.

My African Queen

Take her down to the roaring waters,
steer her up to freedom now.

Sail down the river, Rosie,
sail down my African queen!

Shallow waters won`t ever stop you,
nor stormy winds and rain.

Sail down the river, Rosie,
sail down my African queen!

Fight the calamities all day long,
but fill the nights with love.

Sail down the river, Rosie,
sail down my African queen!

The sun is burning out your soul
and you`r skimmering in fever.

Sail down the river, Rosie,
sail down my African queen!

One day you`ll reach the golden lake
to fight and sink Louisa.

Sail down the river, Rosie,
sail down my African queen!

You rest at the bottom of the sea,
all your dreams have drowned.

Sail down the river, Rosie,
sail down my African queen!

Sail down the river, Rosie,
sail down my African queen!

(Dedicated to Hep` and Bogey)

Smart

One of the elders
took her hand
and prayed with
The unknown preacher.

Pray, preacher, pray

One of the girls
took his hand
and slayed
The unknown preacher

Pray, preacher, pray

Why not?

The vampire walked
alone by night
in the dark forest,
trying to avoid the
killing of a deer
standing in his way.

Why not, why not, why not?

„What's wrong?“
asked the deer.
„I'm vegetarian.“
The deer laughed.
The Vampire began
to kill him softly.

Why not, why not, why not?

„What's wrong?“
asked the deer.

„Sorry boy, I just
Didn't like you!
Never play with a
bad tempered vampire.

Why not, why not, why not?

Go back to Alabama

When you turn the wheel
of your car to go back
to Alabama, never forget
to spit on the floor.

When you turn the heels
of your black boots to
reach Alabama, never forget
to polish them well.

The Sheriff there will
spit on your boots
and will ask you:
„Have a problem, Sir?"

Just say no or you'll be dead
at the end of the day.

The angels are black

Why they paint the angels
white in European churches?

Why the paint the angels
white in African churches?

Angels fly high, so high!
Near to the burning sun
shouldn't they be black?

Growing up

It's to late to hang around
It's to late to run away
It's to late to fly high,
when you are growing up
for more than fifty years.

It's time to find out
that the way to hell
is paved with wishes
of peaople who never
wanted to be grown up.

Low standards

Tasting blood is a
timely business.

Old blood tastes rotten
but is so noble.

Young blood tastes fresh
but is trash.

The Vampire-Conaisseur
prefers middle-aged ladys.

Loveless

Bloody red Roses
Full silvery tears -
A spiny track
Divides the sky.

losing a flower
end up in trash.
clattering steps
Madame removes

Light

Black ink only
And a faint light.

No one laughs here
As the silence screams.

Long distances only
And not a destination.

No one feels the razor
Nothing for deaf ears.

On the bright end
Still no green light.

Quo Vadis

Drifting through forums
Ridiculed by smileys
Caught in files
Dancing on keys

Stepping through portals
Notify my videos
Fresh pixeled scenes
On inkjet postcards.

Browse through lists of links
cracking remote servers
Username Ganymede
Password quo vadis

Pensioner

The young general
stirs his hot coffee
And counts cool
the next
Detonations.

Disordered
by ploughing
the endless
aerial bombs
carve the depths of funnel.

He sniffs
The flowers
And counts rigidly
The dead of the
following Night.

the white
hero crosses

are drawing
Geometricfigures
in the silent park

The old general
Folds his hands
and mumbles
the name of his
Last battle.

Seaside

The old man
silently is sitting
on the beach.

The sparkle of tears,
and the whitecaps
and the blinding sun.
Staring lengthy
into the wide,
no consolation,
not for him.

The old man
is Sitting by the sea
and sighs.

Your heart

The blue stars
are extinguished,
and the sun must
shine.alone -
darkness

On the wings of love
softly you leftme,
to the distant Sea
of the beautiful souls
Gently sweeping.

Your hand in my hand,
our wordless grief
You gave me your heart,
That I should keep it
for the infinite ocean

The black wings
once will carry me

to the distant waves
to return thy heart
And add mine..

Glare

With all the big names
we should be blinded.
Alas, the Princes of the Spirit
Requested unconcerned
Award-winning reverences.

Did you switch of the glare,
old ballerinas turning in the dark
Broken in life and work,
turning last Pirouettes
lull the admirers.

The lost poets

It is up to us
to curse the silent poets,
which have withdrawn
to leave us alone
in the noisy deserts
with Slammers and Rappers.

It is up to us
to call out the lost poets,
who have wrapped up themselves
in their glassy cocoons
of the midnight blue cafes
to the bankers and chillers.

It is up to us
to seek the wild words again,
to suck life from fresh metaphores,
to ignite the new poetic fires,
in the hearts of the singers
dreaming the sounds of children.

Human

The human body consists
Of large amounts of water
And a few minerals
And some tiny
Traces of compassion.
All the rest?
Barely measurable.

Precincts

In infinite sadness
My heart is petrified

Dumbfounded horrors
Paralyzing my steps

Every day I am stumbling
Along the precincts

Encircling myself to
preserve your memory

Harmony

Richly blessed
With precious gifts
The host returns
With empty hands.

The Author

Peter Hardcastle is an accomplished writer and journalist living in France. He has published several mystery novels.

www.peter-hardcastle.de

5231216R10027

Printed in Great Britain
by Amazon.co.uk, Ltd.,
Marston Gate.